rivers of the driftless region

Also by Mark Conway

Dreaming Man, Face Down
Any Holy City

Chapbook

First Body

rivers of the driftless region

Mark Conway

four way books

tribeca

Library of Congress Cataloging-in-Publication Data

Names: Conway, Mark, author.
Title: Rivers of the driftless region / Mark Conway.
Description: New York, NY : Four Way Books, 2019.
Identifiers: LCCN 2018028711 | ISBN 9781945588297 (pbk. : alk. paper)
Classification: LCC PS3603.O56495 A6 2019 | DDC 811/.6--dc23
LC record available at https://lccn.loc.gov/2018028711

This book is manufactured in the United States of America
and printed on acid-free paper.

Four Way Books is a not-for-profit literary press. We are grateful for the assistance
we receive from individual donors, public arts agencies, and private foundations.

This publication is made possible with public funds from the
National Endowment for the Arts

and from the New York State Council on the Arts, a state agency.

We are a proud member of the Community of Literary Magazines and Presses.

for Therese

The driftless region is the corner of southeastern Minnesota untouched by the most recent glaciers. Unlike the rest of the state, there are no glacial deposits, or "drift." The landscape remains as it was thousands of years ago, a jagged terrain of bluffs, deep gorges, and many small fast-running rivers.

contents

rivers of the driftless region

∞

1: as zero to the infinite

2: any fraction of infinity is not finite

3: ∞

4: ...

: as zero to the infinite

. . . experience of the eternal is a kind of death, and the only thing that separates it from real death is that it is not final because no living creature can endure it for any length of time.

Hannah Arendt

in the blizzard

the horses are filthy in their winter coats
grubby and matted
manes mended with hay ::
they shuffle /
heads down—flickering :
limping homeward between
snows like medieval pilgrims: seen
and invisible /
unseen and real . . .
the blizzard continues and the world is the wind
our eyes close to slits
inside the drift and the howl
the horses aren't ours / not even broken to ride
still they help us get home
as we look into the wind
seeing nothing but whiteness ahead
with them dark inside

in the ruins

we drank in the remains of ruined buildings
we sat in caves or wrecked houses
on farms given back to the bank
listening to men who'd been raised
in ways that were lost
we strained to make out the use of their news
they were crazy or passed out white pills
notched on the face with an x or the cross
they drank from the flask and the mouth
they came in and shook off the rain
dismayed and inflamed :: calm and arcane
the least one seethed chanting whitman for hours
then wept at the dregs of the fire
foam formed at the edge of their lips
we drank and looked for something to drop
waiting and sifting for signs
inscribed in black chalk
we were young we were sure
we knew how to die but not how to last
a small man who claimed he was blake
raged all night and probably he was ::
he had god in his sights
white crosses shone in our eyes or maybe bad sunshine—
in the ruins the men talked: seraphic and broken
glowing with knowledge and garbage
we sorted their mad sacred words
these dog-headed guides to the life-after /
and the life after that

in the light

but still down
the plain back road
your un-lived lives hive
and clog the trailing mind . . .
to see as if the light
went right through you :
to hear as if words
went through you :
to see the dream—
to see it's not a dream
of what's to come
but what came . . .
your exhausted breath
is sucked up by the pines
you go on :: breathing
as if you didn't know
you were breathing
walking the road as if
you had no idea what it's like
not to be alive

in a rush

we went down to
the winter garden—nearly
material —
and made time crazy
over our truce:
you were young beautifully
totaled—it was speed
you lived for and returned to
on bent knees / riddled
with needles—
moving faster and
faster / still never—
quite—reaching
break-away speed . . .
of course you had to
slam back into the inevitable
earth :: you left us
your gift of partial
omniscience—we discovered worlds
without end end first
with a pause
that goes on and on

inside the here

frost on the vines—
frost on the fence post
the basil burnt up
the garden more lovely / stripped down
to black
it's good to be thrown down
on the ground / awake in the field—
all the plains
gone in the eyes . . .
zero time : zero times
zero: it's finally now ::
no sound not even atoms
as they spin in white huts
just one thought and all think it
as one:
crow   heifers   hay-bales   small man on his back
all of us / sift into
the deepening wheatfield
swept into the gray waves
we once saw as light

at the end of the year
the children were ground
into december
only to be given a train and some dolls . . .
god grew young:
smelted down—
he reappeared in a cradle of straw / ready to be adored
by a cow; we didn't care
till we knew we'd been renewed
for the new year ::
given life—we ordered the same again and loved it
insanely / again / enthralled
with the views
taped over our screens
we knew a fool
who persists in his folly becomes
angelically huge—
able to lean in to hear
the prophet whispering
the world is a bridge :
pass over it—but build no houses on it ::
he who hopes
for a day may hope for eternity . . .
he told us that:
we who still hope
for everything

in the non-tourist version

I believe in her
suffering
because I believe in
suffering—
these days I hang
from her
like a clapper
from a bell / then
sway :: tongue-
tied / blacked out
in her shade—
she said: this world of yours—
it's dank and
circular ::
I've always said
I need her body
for my pain
to make a sound :: yet . . .
there are times—
in massive afternoons—
you should use
your eyes
out there new lovers
stroke and prod and
then implode—
lids shut tight
to keep
the sights inside

in the only siberia we have near

our half-days looked longer /
folded together—
the burnt corn and straw tender
and torn . . .
you see your children / equidistant in evening
through shoots of ivy
walking up the white stairway
to the stone turret :
lips move . . .
reciting silently
from the hymnal of i-pads
faces shining with knowledge you'll never have
.....
....
give them your war-profits
give them your plow and old sofa
give them your father / who colonized marshes
for tract-housing :: the historical father
who sang on days the winds rose
give him away : now that he loves you
now that he's forgotten the simple forms
of contempt—
now that he's shrunken to enter
the black steppes to come

in the cloister

he mistook cause for the river
the crow for a fable ::
mistook the thing for the thing
it stood for
his lives more real when seen
as a book . . .
he thought he'd improve
by refusing /
machined down: smoothed by experience
and all his old schoolmates—torn
by terrible elations ::
he took silence as approval
white noise as the roar
of the crowd . . .
. . . .
outside the disputed city
he began :: sewing the black hood
of his new order—
—each stitch pulled through the eye
of stiff cotton /
the fabric slipping open . . . there—
and again / not-there
. . . .
. . . .
in the white abbey
I can see him—kneeling—
praying out the seasons:
moving without moving
like lava / alive

11

in the [partially] corrupt version

it was then you were surrounded
by [illegible] trees
and cities spinning
through the helix
of your gravely-hooded gaze
only making your eyes
more totally desired
by the sluttish painter
to paint
after he'd envisioned
licking on them
slowly—bold and
hazel staring through truth and the piazza
though truth be [blank]
most of your limbs
were already thickly an-
notated in the annals
of desire: [expurgated]
hair twisted french into braids /
the azimuth of air swirling
round the sharply-sculpted head—
your profile mirrored
in the painter's glass display case :
a floating image
the laws of optics tell us
can't be tasted :: only wanted—
a dark abstraction painted
on the moving air

in the rooms

x

we know the future / brother
because we know
the weather : always
just the same sun
folded back /
behind the rains . . .
.....
there are certain birds
you can't see /
sister / more than fit inside
the vision—rising
in the morning weather ::
you hear them in
the low skies
smeared above the life raft—
drifting past the wooden
living rooms

xx

all night installed inside
the summer blabber seminars
we yakked it up
in several
dialects of time
then went out
and built a council-

fire / made of
crappy tiki torch
blinking mostly
choking on its own
greasy light ::
I heard your clever
yak yak through
several stanzas
of messianic howling:
the horny dogs of
autumn—
I hung on you—
on each beat
of your lush /
divided mind

xxx

does it matter
that I finally
bathed my father
beneath the black plank ceiling
of his final room?
issa said it's stupid
to wash howling
infants and corpses in the poem
before
they washed him :: here
the clouds came

14

extra low—
so low they brought
the sun down ::
we hardly knew we missed
the skies
we hadn't seen for days

in the pines

the world is fire / again
today: summer pours through
our eyes—ignites
behind the face
of everyone we meet
then glances off
my shining suit-of-light ::
—july—
silkscreened to
the skin . . .
. . . .
the bedroom's flap-flap fan
wastes all
our requisitioned wind :
long-day sun
drinks gin : then burns the dawn to stumps
my four souls lie down—
overheated from the past :
good dogs—they watch me
panting in the shade . . .
children tear through
another week of empty street / make us
trek to hermit's point
where we throw ourselves
into the unspeakable ::
the local unclean lake
. . . .
the small ones—bored—
run up the beach

dripping off their fire ::
here is the new life—burning
like the old life

in a low himalaya

my son breathes to leave me
to leave the lean-to
of family: extended and penal
he leaves to shut his eyes
on the uplands
one among many wandering sitters
who sleep in the rain: gone
in the cascade of first causes . . .
my son washes his hands of the west wind
exhales the sorrows
I gave him
the breathing once hovered over
he rocks back and forth
squinting as he shines in the rain
a rain frail
with potential / total and pale
and unnoticed . . .
closing his eyes / inhaling: he
holds our breath

:   any fraction of infinity is not finite

Elsewhere perhaps, by all means, elsewhere, what elsewhere can there be to this infinite here?

Samuel Beckett

in the air

you sit there—looking at nothing :

waiting for the laptop to steal music

the icon blinks on : meaning: the music will arrive in an eternity

the one starting—now / at the moment of download

the eternity that also means—never ::

the never that's happening now

the little wheel keeps spinning trying to pull impermanence into
             coltrane (a love supreme: the complete masters)

I need coltrane's supreme love for the terminal—

mainly: *pt. IV - psalm -:- live in juan-les-pins/1965*

you sit there / waiting to board and sit around again until greece arrives

then you step into the olive orchard / frail and blind

the icon that is you brightens visibly / before slipping off

to check into a room near the square ::

....

:: the airport people moved the seats—

they want to make us think coltrane will appear and take us to the
        lush life

we slouch in our nightclub plastic chairs and stare into phones /
        hurtling privately toward the end of time—

it's waiting there for all of us to arrive

then we'll have to stand around and talk until history is through :

but the mystics say—"stars and blossoming fruit trees . . . utter
        permanence and extreme fragility give an equal sense
        of eternity"

;- that's simone weil:

utter olive blossoms . . .

in the terminal the customers look down from their outposts

a few raise their shutters to let another person in through the strained
        indoors air / mostly their eyes say: the fuck you looking at?

I'm at home among the non-mystics :: some keep the back door
        slightly ajar

a few wouldn't rule out a quick trip to the fake irish pub

children see us hiding in our minds

I raise my eyebrows the kids laugh because they see I'm slightly real

then close the shutters and go back to my book

I need the olive trees for ballast in the air

I'm about to enter the orchard of the pre-socratics :: fact: I need to
        read the phrase book more

but I get obsessed / watching their ancient heads explode as they
        discover logic

let that be a lesson to us I say to the extremist icon in myself—the one
        who is simone weil

through the terminal air my book talks patiently to me / reciting from
        its single memory:

it tells me the early greeks thought the kosmos was permeated by god—

everything is god inside not-god

that creates a system problem they eventually have to solve :: what if
        god leaks out?

zeno never took a plane though it's clear he waited in a terminal—the
      universe is motionless said zeno to the children

children love a paradox

turns out I had to buy the coltrane—now I own *ascension a love
      supreme* (masters) and *john coltrane/johnny hartman*

coltrane believed in motion / his notes blued and molten—even I can
      hear that in my icon ears

we keep hurtling toward friday soaked in the odor of our metaphysics
      —the airport lounge discolored by our flame

the airport's voice says—we're bound to climb

....

we non-mystics start to level off / in-flight vision screens turned on

it appears the greeks carved eternity in two—the never-ending and
      what's outside time

in the never-ending we degrade at constant rates set mercifully to
      a speed we can't detect

in our hearts we know: we can't keep this up

the plane catches us in the paradox of midair / the backroom full of
      salted nuts ::

I rise up above my skin / look down at my moving self :: seems
      apparent I should have something better to do . . .

logic says: should have purchased more leg room

me and the non-mystics watch our flight path over greenland while we
      decay at speed

we want eternity / just not now . . .

utter simone weil

....

truth is: this isn't my first quest-rodeo

last year I turned east—trying to download eternity from the
      mountain sages

I want to taste it once more before I go / even if it's largely self-induced

last year my boxed set told me asia had a huge headstart on the greeks

the ricepaper whispered as I turned the pages / the father-sages
      distilling mountains into silence

looking down through the condensation of the tiny porthole I spied
        their rivers

they have water-eyes ::

they sit in driftless rivers undivided from the clouds

drenched / they look up laughing : shu shih says:

my answer is
a wine cup / full of the
moon drowned in the river

....

the air over southern europe is completely rigid

it's getting dimmer / post-atlantic :: the greeks still mumbling logic in
        their sleep :

they toss and turn inside eternity with another one just outside

darkness pours through the empty gate

I open my laptop / the download spinning in its homemade wind

the monitor glances up at me / says: time remaining: -00-

music loops through silver curves of ∞ / coiling through the spheres of
    earth-imported air

the hourglass icon siphons sand :: sifts it back

mystics belly-laugh at in-flight dialogue unheard beyond their buds

flight attendants know the unspoken / mercifully bring beer

I crank up my paid-for music : coltrane and johnny hartman's lush life
    in my ears . . .

those come what may places

where one relaxes on the axis of the wheel of life—to get the feel of life

from jazz and cocktails :

I'm pretty sure the attendant heard me / mind-singing: I'll live a lush life

in some small dive / and there I'll be—while I rot with the rest . . .

the eternal—just beyond our skin ::

the elders—way behind me—drift in empty boats

streams rise into mists—river-sages float / indivisible in water-time

utter river ::

I mind-sing to shu shih / tell him: even mainly empty / I was here

....

we fall through the western air / at the proper angle to decay

rains come down in tongues muttering retsina and mud

I read the book faster / desperate for an exit while god leaks
        systemically through the west

europe rises: lush and porous . . .

we the airborne have been deprived of trays—

I look down : my body-icon—seriously trashed

it settles mostly immobile in the seat below my mind

the pilot tell us we've returned from just below the ancient void

: / doesn't matter / really :: fact is: we can't move

shuffling / stumbling dimly through sub-lunar aisles

we descend on moving stairways : the self immobile—

though too immense to see / the firmament pulses in our eyes

27

we blink and rest : rinsed of june 12 2015—

all around us the music spins invisibly at speed

I slump down in the crowded bus / hurtling through myself

the streets throb lyrically and hum :

ahead the ancient city blinks :: utter heat and stone

in a good man

eternity looks through time
in the death of a good man
Goethe

we don't see the glass—
but the sand
through the neck of the hourglass
time falling through
the forms. . . .
goethe wasn't really such
a good man—and yet
we see right through him :
he wrote his transparent words
the same year
blake burned
his prophecies in acid baths
to tell us eternity's
in love with time . . .
so we live on
in ice-sheds / in houses made of wind ::
eternity looks through us
like fishermen through water :
we're seen
eating in the kitchen
proving we're not good—
much too visible
beneath the radiance
of the covering sky
for the good man is a clear man /

solid in his barn :
he magnifies the work of grain
seen through
the bottle of his neck
he turns the dirt to wheat
grinds himself to glass

in total retreat

at the mind spa
the voice-box turned off /
a relief
to put down the song-wheel the talk-talk ::
I had to be out of my mind
to think of my mind . . .
still the eyes
always busy—out
collecting lais and red curries
my eye-skin in miami taking in bankers
wretchedly half-naked / parasailing
:: I sit back / delete
the flasher the rude waiter the blank-faced girl sailor ::
but the eye-wheel
keeps spinning the light into chowder and saris
look it:
I drive off the grounds
seeing long-billed alabamans putting
on surfaces green as money
for money ::
I'm the breath man—
double-lungs chopping and chewing the cud
of white space
into mindfully-slowed breathing . . .
my breath rises into white wheels—
gusts shaking the meadows
back into barley

in the high days

those were the weeks
of my pre-conversion—
the sun clear as cider / preserving
the late light of september . . .
roads led to roads down to lanes
and dark cities
to taverns bursting with
bow-legged women and pork swimming
in au jus—
it was then I'd such longing
for the undoing of seasons
taking down summer's hair
smelling her unblemished cotton . . .
behind my motives
I saw nothing
but hunger and went on—
as the young do—
lifting down the night bottle
taunting the stars as nothing / nothing but holes
that town made me
swore me
to be done with the long burn / I converted
my mysterious mind
into water / made it clear as the night lying
on cornfields ::
summer evenings
the moon rises
tearing my old thoughts off
almost as though
they never made me

in a sense

it's easier—erased—
to see the tongue inside
the flame
and hear the prairie breathe
slumped in roadside ditches
smoking handrolled / waiting for the ride
that never came ::
I gave up and took the dog-bus
across the crushed face
of both dakotas . . .
now—in this barest room—
I trance and leave the bazaar behind to clerks and thieves ::
I leave to hear the prairie move
. . . .
the torture torturers like best
is not to let you sleep:
you see visions but
of the hidden face
it's better not to . . .
in the hospice of the prophet
you'll be given knowledge
of the melting stones that feed the maple / help them
meet the clouds . . .
the dying are given visions:
seven nights of pleasure
then the blizzard—
the upturned faces
filling up with snow

in a state

riding rivers alluvial and urinal
down to the delta—
you came back to us / camoed
in kohl
then talked to yourself
in hit lyrics
mumbling to q-tips / lip-synching to spoons:
so now meister-singer   sing us—
in plainsong—sing up
the bog and the prairies
where po-faced mud farmers
live on subsidized mush:
sing up the cottonwoods filling the flat air
making it white
with weed seedlings—
bring back the days before
you took the dayjob
when you lived easy in the stink
of barn-swabbing
and doctored the milk with a whole jug of bleach—
sing with your gray tongue
singalong with . . . wait . . . there now—
you hear them?
let's rejoin the hunters
where ancient hound dogs
wail over losing
treed raccoons to their sons

imao

don't lie to me like that—
tell me the new lies:
tell me we'll grow to love
the stubby fingers of the gruppen-leader
that the longing for the homeland
is better than being there—
tell me the poorly-stuccoed sky
means: there is no other side
and the lifting mist reveals more
than ground-up vials of crack ::
say it: our brother isn't null
we have flowers in our hair
tell us the mind
isn't a scale-model for the sky : :
. . .
some gods exist
to take up space—
days are long / somehow more
like amputated limbs: what you feel
is phantom pain :
thoughts are small
to fit inside your head ::
remember you were you
back when you were
just a boy

in my (back-up) religion

truth is:
my religion's self-
inflicted:
I admire lot's woman
who turned to salt when shown
what she'd done;
I too seep double-saline—eating crackers
hidden behind
laundry doors :: there I feel it:—
big-presence: the low barometric
of the huge one
lowering himself over my mouth / he is—
breathing along . . .
I've got to tell you:
my sadness is sad—and now:
all is ended—
sealed like a sandwich;
I trust it
as far as the ham goes :: thing is
I laugh at my girlfren who sits
with her girlfren
huffing the gases of springtime
the scent somehow makes them both gladder:
well:
let them—the stench
will become them—
coating their insides with
the unmistakable spring fragrance
of lilacs and trash

cult rivers of the northern driftless

when I saw the cranes
and learned of my obsolescence—
the covered figures
on the fires at dawn—
with all of us
(body without end /
soul of the species)
all of us knowing
we'd be cradled by the belly
then released
into the cult rivers of the driftless—
it came to me :
that this was only
yesterday: and I was in the middle
of my own life ::

when I saw the cranes
and learned of my obsolescence
I saw the replacement armies
going up the mountains literally
body without end soul of the species
into the future perfect—
the present burning
in the furnace of the mind :
the troops / swaddled
in mud—slogging ahead
in the open moment . . .

when I saw the cranes
and learned my adolescence
has been planned well
in advance—
the humiliating locker-
room spectacles
the shop teacher with plastic breath /
back-handed crotch-
chafes by the prelate—
all to soften up
the youth of my century
so we'd do anything
to reproduce our obsolescence—

to endure the jock hairnets
of upperclassmen
rabbit punches
of the wrestling coach—
just so we would mate
in the backseats
of the family's lordly ford falcon
first given glimpses
of the suggestively swollen features
of the other species—flash
of slit and
tongue

when I saw the cranes
and grandstands of the viewing parties
and felt my body without end
seep into sweetwater
I ebbed into the current /
felt myself erode
into waveform
leaking toward the dream
of the mind-without-end—
even as I felt myself
released into
its cloud of knowing
holding us and knowing us
as we faltered /
smoked by the waters—

it was then I began to recede into the driftless—
felt myself lifted
and saw in my mind
every inch of my cultic river's
black banks
the length of the streambed
with all of us
sucked into whitewater
pulled through the widening dissolve

: ∞

(on memory) *Even though it is part of my nature, I cannot understand all that I am. This means, then, that the mind is too narrow to contain itself entirely.*

St Augustine

in the acceptable infinite

they went down
to see the mother—hidden
in a cloud of fur
and potpourri:
she's old now / she's only
in her mind
she who'd previously been louise
she went on
humming something something in the deficit
of tenses—changing slowly back
into the changeless
she who'd been
so careful saving everything
for the plural afternoons
she'd sit swirling on the open porch
withered and
clear as the girl
she still sees at night
swinging through the sycamores :
crows rustle black
sheet-metal wings—
her mother crying out . . .
waiting to be born

in the museum of the prairie

synonyms for the sky? :: none;
we had the one bowl
over our heads
leading to the useless horizon—
re-enactors sat on their hands
hands that wept
through canvas gloves / then grew hard as the plow
built for corn : we toured
the architect's model of the sky :: obviously
inspired by god's terrible
childhood in north dakota—long afternoons where eternity grew
we learned to search
for mesas or oases
any break in the backdrop
but the trick is
you have to look closer / into the wheat's bearded skull:
eventually . . .
you'll rise ::
meanwhile / listen
to the field harps and sky harps ring
ecstatically off-
key

in one more day

her eyes reflower in the storm
of birds: here another spring :: so what
survived must live—
dirt-bike girls lay tracks of noise ::
we barely hear the trees
colonize new soil:
they drive all day for
their daily loaf of dirt
.....
....
the golden souks of men suck up
what was once our sun
march it back to town
make it get to work :
her eyes reform the birds
......
wind crawls through the rifled field
looking for a place to fall :
our fathers sleep in wounds
stand in single file and testify
they were not the man ::
elders drive alberta down
to her shores of mud
then meet for tonic-ed gin
the sun sings like electric trains :
drips like yellow gravy :
our fathers sleep in wounds

painted faces pretty much stove-in :
flowers storm her eyes
re-colonized by birds

war world

he was older
than my father: my father
younger than the war
and the face
he wore to combat:
vacant : thin as kafka :
awol in the church
behind the lines
praying for the mercy
whistling through
the flemish air
like shrapnel . . .
my old man: beneath
the frozen ardennes—
rawer than the starving
offspring of the krieg
strafers barely teenage . . .
younger than the brother
killed in the distant
theater he'd seen
featured in the newsreel:
iwo jima—
the handsomest pilot who never lived
as far as I'm concerned
died before the war
was done and I
watched the reenactments
late at night as reruns
when I was young . . .

when I was older
than my father
the corpsman / kneeling
in the chapel
when the m p's
lift him—lightly—
lead him back
into the zone

in the first bird

rain pours down our inner
darkened streets:
my unenlightenment / finally /
nearly done ::
I hear the mind of god
is open to the south—
even trees fly
in the wind
and time is on our side—
I heard that
in the scarecrow church—the one that sleeps headdown ::
way above the opened ground
the sun hides inside
a double coat of chrome—
...
....
my father came back
inside a bird—
the cardinal sexed in red ::
he chose it
to represent his piety—
we see it move like his wet mouth almost
every night
then fly off at dusk ::
he lets go
a knotted chord of notes

spreads his wings with grace:
all this from
that grief-struck man who once
lumbered on this earth

in his chair—electric

sirloin chugs toward my father's heart
as he sits out in the garden;
rods throb through
the cataracts that guard his eyes—
he sits on charged electrons
coursing through his electric chair
on his last tour through
the atomic life of objects
he rides his chair as maples
slide open into leaves :
he's total
for the moment / nearly
equal to the dark ::
fused into the recliner—
the neighbors can't tell
man from chair . . .
my father: the centaur:
half-man / half-furniture
his eyes fill
with chlorophyll—green tea
of spring he drinks
through shattered irises . . .
a blur at dusk
atoms shake him
in their mouth / he shivers through the dark
like a human hive

in the disease that is ending

no one told him
his chemo would make him clairvoyant
at least in predicting
small changes of light
he saw the phases of his children
darken after weeks at the seaside—
took pleasure
in the glow that hung
in the air of the sterilized bedroom
the hot days spooling off
of their aggregate skin
....
he watched them / amazed—
not at how fast
the sun left their faces
but how easily
they let it go

in the aftermath

after him the bedroom sagged—
the wallpaper peeled like fruit;
after his canoe went past
wild rice wove the way back shut
hiding his last way through;
acids made a shroud of gas
his face became cement . . .
after him the mallards whistled in unafraid
of his gray gun /
acids made a shroud ::
after him the gases raced like gnats—
mallards whistled in
his photo grayed like
his old remington . . .
after him our prayers flew up
like shot into the middle sky /
the children drew their prayers with pens;
wavy lines stood in
for the speed we couldn't see :
his eyes lay heavily at rest
after him the stories stayed lost inside the north
after him his brother broke the seal
and lay there drinking last-man scotch
acids made a shroud
his face gray as the wildest rice
after him a transparent cloud of gas
followed for a while
after him / then trailed off

in the night ships

x

came to at the entrance to a field
filled with wheat / broken pillars—
closed for the season—
the grain black / gleaming with rot
thin soil trickling to the shore . . .
the children arrived in waves / singing
their lessons their koans
mouths taped shut; put on boats back to where they came from
it's almost like they're still alive . . .

xx

we gathered we lived in the middle of the field
now and at the hour of nightmare:
the children aware they are drowning
aware of the water we put in the lungs of their fathers
by now they know they were complicit
of occurring in war and on water
the children-in-question could have been born anywhere
some were known to be part of the ocean
most were aware they'd have to go back
the sea is large so they travel en masse
not all could get through we were aware
that was part of the plan
they know the way home and the sea
the seas are unusually calm

xxx

the questionable children lie in the huts drinking the air :
their parents stagger on sea legs
the ground like water under their feet
they're buried in sand until after lunch
their feet bound in the way we feel is traditional
we bind them folded over
we code the soles of their feet the back of their hands
having come across water we put them in water
they prove they're refugees by refusing to swim
they insist they're not refugees yet sleep in the sand
they prove they're not thirsty by refusing to drink
we set them back in the water : they turn into waves

in a decent imitation

of end-times: nothing
happens . . .
officials shuffle room-
to-room strip-
searching strangers with skill
and indiscretion :
we wake up feeling
amazing in the morning after
knowing the end
first appears—ultra-
normal / only
more so . . .
the vista opens
to an aperture that shatters
into music
the horizon holding all
we've ever seen
ever wanted to see—
there:
before our very very eyes

in the seven stages of creating the gods

we worshipped first
old men: mainly the fire
in their heads—
we revered the lore they knew
and wrung the sparrow's neck
to help them read the gut for signs ::
we were slammed across the head
to make our thoughts line up to bow ::
they had us eat
the private workings of the hog
and tied our tongues with cloth ::
we came to love the silence
hoarded in a bell . . .
certain youths were forced
to dance inside their mouths
we went in to golden doges—faces
plush with drink—
and watched them sweat
through flowing silk . . .
we drew interest from the sky ::
a magistrate cleared our minds of hate
by filling us with kerosene
then they made us close our eyes
to help us imitate
the end of days

ingrate

gave us the sickness of visions
made me a mystic:
clairvoyant / but boring—
turned a blind eye
as long as our insights
rendered us useless ::
here in the coming of ages
we've come into this one / holding our breath
in the long fall
and failure of evening
and: you gave us
the times of our lives
known as "the time of our lives" . . .
gave us the chutzpah to wake up
in mecca in kyoto
with heartbroken rotors
you saved us
the trouble of leaving by leaving
you gave us the drought of your face

in the eye

this townie world's
skinniest genius
and heiress:
left eighty-five acres stripped of topsoil—
cut up and sold off
as sod ::
her dingy father taught her
the art of dirt-farming
how to pick potatoes
mashed later
to be ladled out
to the seasonal hands
now she finds herself / falling
through the courtrooms
of bismarck / back where
her father was bred:
leonard
the counterfeit mystic—
required by law
to return her each monday
to the mother who wept
through curtains of dust . . .
each morning she
catches herself / staring
into her own eyes
as they gaze back in the mirror . . .
she can't look away—
seeing life

quiver

did it change
your posture—
that being
ah / that being under
rapture?
do you feel it still
ah feel it's still
a lesser form
of clairvoyance—
the ecstatic?
your face slack /
thrown open
until you return

as practice
you admit
it's a little ironic / slash /
masochistic—
a taste of what
you can have only
when you're no longer you—
we go on
through serial moments
mostly anti-
ecstatic / fingering
player pianos in
descending scales ah
un-fucking-
fulfilling / agreed

in the eloquent absence
of rhap-
sodic panting
upright / insensible
in the ah sensate
surround : come on
face it—you weren't
really twisting
in the changeling ah
unchanging
wind :: not even
levitating / merely
unrisen while hidden
stars moaned through
their holes

you lay essential
as ocean
the waves centered
in making ah
unmaking the mesh
of air we breathe
through :: / clearly
you felt it—
the updraft
that curled slightly
your fingers—
I wonder: did it alter
their grasping nature

as they closed
on nothing
then relaxed—only
to open like oceans /
pre-wave?

out of the blue

she wrote straight out
of the côte d'azur
to let me know she'd come through
un-helped / unseen
then told me
how I am—she herself
is scathed but good
at healing;
her adopted farm
stores its choicest cheese in caves
to rot a bit—
huge wheels of cream
improved by dark experience—
she said that
once or twice
as she rocked inside the hull / carried
by the waves /
she thought of us—
our bareback rides to hermit pond:
so new and raw
we could be seen
clear through—the way
her neighbors lift
and check a glass
of just-poured wine

in the last world

it's cold inside
the rubber torso of the gecko
stuck on the wall
of the southern living room . . .
it has to wear that face
till spring :
it's cold in the gecko legs
cold in the climate-changed hollers—
natural history burns
out in the backyard:
smudge-fires lit to save
the drowsing lime trees
carpets of mosquitoes seep
in sullen pools and scheme till noon:
they are time ::
they will conquer all:
in the kitchen
it's always rice—
the yankee cook grins with grease
deflowers the frog for legs
he sets them in the pan
to steep: they relax
and float and as the last world warms
they jerk

on the sidewalk / suddenly bowing

not bowing / really—
more : doubled-
over / maybe choking ::
that's the one time
I stop long enough to bow
to the honored moment—
the one I keep on missing . . .
but now / tripping
on the broken sidewalk
I bow to the infant
I once was / bow
to the child-actor who played me
to the young man smoking in the pines / watching . . .
I bow to my brothers—
the ones who've taken up the work of time—
bow lower to my mother
as she parts the curtains—
sees in my eyes the great mysteries . . .
that it's me who will bring the last one to her room

in the driftless

I'm older—over
there—sleeping :: partially
decaying / taken up

in night sweats
as mind solvent drips
through padded caves ::

it gets me twitching /
deep in dream-
raging—I forget

I've never forgiven
(really) any of them: them
dumb bastards :

with both of us dying
together daily / crazy
at the home movies

unreeling in our heads
where we're always
young   we live forever

through fiestas in
muggy a.m.'s / our aging
recorded at the atm

we're seen: daily :
inhaling money:
otherwise oblivious

we float through
the driftless region—
weightless / daily

as mayflies / inside
their time that
never passes:

the moment
just lifts them
an instant / then

goes on / untwisting . . .
you see us—
riding streams

faces veiled
in nets of insects / infinite
in their droning—

the long evening

suspended—
draped over

dark broken waters—
the past always
in us / as river /

spilling down to
the ocean . . .
looking back

into the black west
we're in it / again
the driftless

: . . .

It's easier for me to see everything as one thing than to see one thing as one thing.

Antonio Porchia

∞   ∞   ∞   ∞

in the rear-view

i

now the world :
the world in the glare
of the world / hidden
inside its dark shining—
the way a bird
smashes into
our picture window / falling
for a more
luminous sky : it's true
I saw you
in the unfurling
sails / diving off
the wharf after selling out
the whale tour . . .
in now :: is now :
still I saw you
inside the shining . . .
you only see
the earth's curve
from the sky or
sprawled across the waterline
eyes riding up
the breaking wave

ii

the bird in the bird
singing
the outer bird wants
to sing—too :
my hand
my old hand
turns into
my old hand :
the road singing dirt . . .
two days before they died
the people I knew
memorized the room
by looking in my eyes—
fading dutch interior
reflecting back . . .
they smile / nodding
at the hum of the emptying room
then turn—
whispering to those already gone
and turn again
to the last face loved
loved though the face
of someone they
no longer know

iii

the world in the finch
seed in the mouth . . .
I see what
you see—to the side
we're lost inside
one mind
I meet you in the infrequent . . .
I want to meet you
in the infrequent clearings :
such a relief
to know you can appear ::
the faces behind what I see—
seeing inside . . .
these days I measure
time by hand
the seen time unrolls
as pause / falls from
the finch beak—
half-hull whirling
to the ground

iiii

I took you down
to the quayside
that was you (infrequent—
flickering near the water)
I talked to beneath
the bitter gulls—
looking back across
the tidal sand
your eyes like the sun
light up the mostly-
visible world : squinting through
the live mirage . . .
your sunlike eyes
look out the mind
looks in

iiiii

children call
to the hawk
now the red hawk :
I hear the glacier
calving to
the north :
also: next-door neighbors eating pizza / talking shit
I know I sleep but
not how I got through
sleep's draped rooms
now day—trees (again) (first off)
sap in the outer ring
as sugar—spring
and the great waters
spin

iiiiii

now the spring :
here the trees
divide in waves
we walk for miles : in our minutes
we remain . . .
the fields move
like the river
moves through rain :
we cut across grainfields
part the green wheat
leave it
broken and supreme
I carry stones
in my shoes / stones
of mud road
the birds alone
can make me sing
I sing: dirt road

iiiiiii

time to move—
I go on
with my father
who was never
my father / always walking farther
off with the sun
in his eyes
eyes we got for day
blindness for night
we can hear
the earth turn at evening
the fire burning down...
if we take the river
we can make it back
by dawn

iiiiiiiii

now the air :
I believe in cold water—
believe that was you—
youthful by the quayside
heaving to . . .
I came to you so
long ago
our civilization now worn
to ruins...
looking in the rear-
view mirror
blinded by the glare—
we see everything
we had is gone :: or lost—
the only thing
we'd planned

in wheat :: the revelator

gray air above
the hayfield sags
then whips—cross-
grain—over
the freezing plains :: never
an end to re-vision . . .
sitting on the front porch
we look through
the unseeable
the air filling with wind /
bright with particulate . . .
the endless prairies last
for ever / then
are rendered to coal :: look—
across the black-canvas sky
past the terrestrial dark
all the lost buffalo
up in flames

in its thin helmet

mystic the wheat straw / beheaded
and baled—bled out and
piled on the cart ::
the sun sits in its high chair /
swollen in light
I haven't eaten for days
what I've seen—
the wind winds in groves of red maples / then dozes:
in my living head
the last days repeat / then go on /
repeating:
mystic the dung spread over the sweetcorn
mystic the seed / the cold rain and twine
mythic the boots—covered in compost
mythic the soft mouths of barn rats
gorging on corn
....
my mind lies awake inside
its thin helmet—
all day / it drinks up—electric / floating
in bone
but you don't need a mind
to see the small girl
down by the lakeside—
mystic the willows that weep in her shallows
mystic the waters that show her her face

in the flagrant night

he lay letting
ideas wash over him
like low-level opiates—
(the minor gods
of oblivion)
ways to make the mind
a tourist of the self . . .
he thought his thoughts
were him—
he'd nod off / timesick
stumbling toward
the fog of his best country :
sleeping :
he liked emotions—like drugs
they never changed him :
he indulged grief in
its over-all schema:
wave forms of hysterias
nerve diseases he listened to
like mahler : music
he didn't get
but became obsessed with
the pain voice
singing *I am lost*
to the world...

he sent himself selfies
until he become
brilliant :: apparent

moments lasting nearly
as long as the crash
of tequila—
they were just feelings
he sampled :
he didn't have—
....
when he was me
I felt everything
move too fast / my life doubled
by regret :: I lived first
through all
that had to change : then
through what could not

in the lee

I trusted
no one / not
that I
blame them /
but now
you—you
stay here
in rooms
filled with
books and
the smoke
of old
music—all
lived in
the eye
of the world-
storm ::
but never
before and no
one ever
stayed here
now even
the days
change
before you

in the exit wound

the gray cat prays
near her station—
the low-lying feeder—
seeing birds as food
come down from the trees;
the doe in our corn
hides at the edge of the treeline . . .
I read over and over
the same page:
friends who have gone
come back by rearranging words I misread
as their names . . .
the invisible isn't improved
by the seen:
each day I don't see you I see you—
head down / out in the garden
your hoarse end-voice
turned into the marsh-call of blackbirds . . .
now let's listen—
my red-winged companions—
as you sing us
the wound of our exit

inside the infinite head of wheat

the germ met the seed in the sex
of the bee come to devour
the wheat's newly-
spun pollen—
a worker swollen
by spring and desire / ready to die
when the job's done . . .
cottonwoods throw
a shawl over the night—
deer rise from their knees
slipping away from
the longhouse of grass :
the grains sing for tonight
they grow green
tomorrow they're threshed
now they sway—
bent at the waist / wave
on one stem
as the wind drones
its long dirge

invisible skies

in shirtsleeves we sing
sparrow hymns ::
we sing
to glorify the grass . . .
at last / the fields
are plain enough
to see . . .
the old man spoke
beyond the wall—
said the master said the world ends
with the rising chest:
your last in-
breath—that's the one
you hold ::
so: creation is
the conspiracy to make it all again—
as it was before
the sparrow sings
its song
revealing skies

in the miniature garden

small eternities slip
across lily pads
and leak in real-time
down temporal bamboo:
my eternal son is here
tearing pages from the book of days
before his father leaves . . .
we're killing time—still—
there's not time for tours:
we lose the guide
double back to see
the garden in the garden
we missed
the first time through:
it's visible—now—
our eyes adjusted to the shade:
curving rows of
withered grasses—
blue and abstract
like the past ::
and the path we cut across—
we never were:
the ferns we crushed
sway and drift /
again / above
the floating ground

in the barely unbearable

I fear most the most beautiful
the city up in flames
the chanting figure's hair on fire
our horizon lit with prophecies and wings
of the tall birds who look after us
I fear those I love
the beauty that can harm them
into seeing / I fear the girl—
fear her feasting on the sight
of seeing fire /
fire I fear the most fire I love
the most for the beauty of its loss
its purity of fear
I fear most the most beautiful
the city struck with flames
the chanting figure's mind on fire
the horizon filled with gantries :: blackened wings
of the large birds that clean up after us
I fear I love the fear
of fire / fear the love
of the loss of—
I fear most the love of
fire—the beauty I can't stand

in the remaining

dreaming of summer—
it's summer ::
the lake slips inside
the doubling skies
pulls them down
to the pines :
in the aftershock of silence . . .
but there is no silence ::
now: honeysuckles
shoot their cream
inside the intricate beaks
of hummingbirds
hovering above
their blurred and honeyed lives ::
we're away from men
beetles rise in peace while the air
weighs less
then less
the pines drift off—blaze
and liquefy . . .
we couldn't help
but find it
beautiful: the earth
sick and soon to die
...
children see the world
has ended
many times:

all the bridges falling—
and—falling—
they keep falling down . . .
midsummer :
sunset—it's early
in the end of days :
apo—"without"
calypse—to "cover"
apocalypse : un-covered : all
falls down
now that we can see . . .
in our eyes
the night's the sky's the lake
is falling through

on the bayou

where the fish were bent—
thinking they're saved
by light curving
through the shallows'
upper stories :
waves dissolve
the silhouettes
drifting beneath
the fish hawk—
out / circling—
before it drops /
turning into
the living light ::
off the bay the creek begins
its clarity / sways off
in a twisting sling of mud . . .
we drift through a hole
into the prairie—
a culvert of metallic cold—
pulled by the current's
slowly beating heart :
at the end of the hollowed dark
trees burn in a pyre of light :
the fire-world
of noon : we ride on the water-air
back into the flames—
on the surface of the green green earth
the only things we see through
and still see

Go blind today already:

eternity too is full of eyes—

Paul Celan

Notes

"in other words": cf. William Blake's *Proverbs of Hell*, "If the fool would persist in his folly he would become wise."

The quotation starting, *"the world is a bridge . . . "* is from an inscription in Fatehpur Sikri, a 16th century city outside Agra, India. Verses from the Quran are inscribed into an archway, the Gate of Victory. The passage quoted is written in Persian and translates as, "Isa (Jesus), son of Mary said: 'The world is a bridge, pass over it, but build no houses upon it. He who hopes for a day, may hope for eternity; the world, though, lasts only an hour. Spend it in prayer for the rest is unseen.'"

"in the rooms": the last section cribs from Robert Hass's *The Essential Haiku,* off-quoting from what Hass notes as Issa's death poem:

     a bath when you're born,

a bath when you die,

how stupid.

"in a good man" misquotes from William Blake's *Proverbs of Hell*, "Eternity is in love with the productions of time."

"in the air": "stars and blossoming fruit trees . . . utter permanence and extreme fragility give an equal sense of eternity" is from Simone Weil's "Chance" in *Gravity and Grace*.

The poem from Shu Shih is the version translated by Kenneth Rexroth in *One Hundred Poems from the Chinese*.

The lyrics to *Lush Life* are from the Billy Strayhorn version as performed by John Coltrane and Johnny Hartman.

"in the driftless": "black west" is lifted from Hopkins.

Acknowledgments

Grateful acknowledgement is made to editors of the magazines and
websites in which versions of these poems first appeared:
2River, Academy of American Poets *Poem-a-Day*, *American Poetry
Review, Colorado Review, Field, Fifth Wednesday Journal, Green
Mountains Review, Kenyon Review Online, A New Ulster* (Northern
Ireland), *Nine Muses Poetry* (Wales UK), *Ploughshares, Poetry Northwest,
Provincetown Arts, Rhino, Southwest Review, Tupelo Quarterly* and
Virginia Quarterly Review.

"in the blizzard" was reprinted in *Desperate Literature: An Anthology*
from the Unamuno Festival, Madrid.

And, to the many friends who looked these poems over, and over and
over, my deep, deep gratitude, especially to Marie Howe, Nick Flynn,
Brenda Hillman, Fanny Howe, Jeff Shotts, Olena Kalytiak Davis, John
Ruff and Spencer Reece, along with huge thanks to Martha Rhodes,
Ryan Murphy and the crew at Four Way Books. Thanks beyond
thanks for constant inspiration and the fact of your presence to the
Conways: Genjô Sam, Cullen and Liam; to the Brown-Conways: Fionn,
Siobhán, Máiréad and Autumn; and to the Nierengarten: Therese; with

gratitude for time, or space, or even time/space, to the MacDowell Colony; the Corporation of Yaddo; Sanskriti Foundation, New Delhi; Galerie Huit, Arles; Xochi Quetzal Writer's Residency, Chapala, Mexico; Glenstal Abbey, Limerick; New Zealand Pacific Studio; Zhong Jie in Chongqing, the McKnight Foundation; the Minnesota State Arts Board and for crucial help on the time/space/bacon-saving continuum, Yelena Tuzova in Moscow and Edgar Mwangi in Nairobi.

"in a blizzard" is for Nick, "in the light" for Marie, "in the air" for Brenda, "in a low himalaya" for Sam, "in the miniature garden" for Liam, "on the bayou" for Cullen and "in the rear-view" for Therese

Mark Conway is the author of three books of poetry. His poems have appeared in *The Paris Review, Slate, The American Poetry Review, Ploughshares, PBS NewsHour, The Kenyon Review On-line, Harvard Review, Bomb* and the Academy of American Poets *Poem-a-Day* series, along with critical essays in the *Oxford Encyclopedia of American Literature*. He has received fellowships from the McKnight Foundation, Jerome Foundation, the Corporation of Yaddo and the MacDowell Colony. He lives north of the driftless region in the Avon hills of Minnesota.

Publication of this book was made possible by grants and donations. We are also grateful to those individuals who participated in our 2018 Build a Book Program. They are:

Anonymous (11), Sally Ball, Vincent Bell, Jan Bender-Zanoni, Kristina Bicher, Laurel Blossom, Adam Bohanon, Betsy Bonner, Mary Brancaccio, Lee Briccetti, Jane Martha Brox, Carla & Steven Carlson, Caroline Carlson, Stephanie Chang, Tina Chang, Liza Charlesworth, Andrea Cohen, Machi Davis, Marjorie Deninger, Patrick Donnelly, Charles Douthat, Emily Flitter, Lukas Fauset, Monica Ferrell, Jennifer Franklin, Helen Fremont & Donna Thagard, Robert Fuentes & Martha Webster, Ryan George, Panio Gianopoulos, Chuck Gillett, Lauri Grossman, Julia Guez, Naomi Guttman & Jonathan Mead, Steven Haas, Lori Hauser, Mary & John Heilner, Ricardo Hernandez, Deming Holleran, Nathaniel Hutner, Janet Jackson, Rebecca Kaiser Gibson, David Lee, Jen Levitt, Howard Levy, Owen Lewis, Sara London & Dean Albarelli, David Long, Katie Longofono, Cynthia Lowen, Ralph & Mary Ann Lowen, Jacquelyn Malone, Fred Marchant, Donna Masini, Catherine McArthur, Nathan McClain, Richard McCormick, Victoria McCoy, Britt Melewski, Kamilah Moon, Beth Morris, Rebecca Okrent, Gregory Pardlo, Veronica Patterson, Jill Pearlman, Marcia & Chris Pelletiere, Maya Pindyck, Megan Pinto, Taylor Pitts, Eileen Pollack, Barbara Preminger, Kevin Prufer, Vinode Ramgopal, Martha Rhodes, Peter & Jill Schireson, Jason Schneiderman, Jane Scovel, Andrew Seligsohn & Martina Anderson, Soraya Shalforoosh, James Snyder & Krista Fragos, Ann St. Claire, Alice St. Claire-Long, Dorothy Tapper Goldman, Robin Taylor, Marjorie & Lew Tesser, Boris Thomas, Judith Thurman, Susan Walton, Calvin Wei, Bill Wenthe, Allison Benis White, Elizabeth Whittlesey, Rachel Wolff, Hao Wu, Anton Yakovlev, and Leah Zander.